The Queen of Brighton

by

Ró Bodley

THE QUEEN OF BRIGHTON
By Ró Bodley
Published by CBS Green Man Publications, in May 2018,
on behalf of Invisible Voices of Brighton & Hove,
as part of the Invisible Voices programme
for the 2018 BRIGHTON FRINGE FESTIVAL.
ISBN: 9789082783636
(NUR CODE 373)
Author: Ró Bodley (RM Bodley)
Editor: Nils Visser
Cover image & interior images
by Marianna Dissing Bjerglys

In Memory of:

Michael Arthur Bodley (Faith Never Shaken)

James Fitzpatrick (Brother)

Contents

Introduction

My journey to Brighton started in September 2015. I decided to come down for a weekend. On the Friday I met a few people and we exchanged numbers.

Saturday morning I spent walking on the beach and became enchanted like many, by the ruins of the west pier. I had seen it many years ago. I started to write as I walked, then stopped at the pump room for a coffee. Then as I walked passed it again, I chatted with a few of the photographers that seemed equally mesmerised and shared my writings with them.

As I sat on the wall editing what I'd written a few hours later, I got a phone call from Anthony who I'd met the previous day. He told me about an open mike event in Cascade Coffee shop on Baker Street. I found myself there reciting the poem I'd written that day "The Queen of Brighton". It was received very well and always has been. It seems right and fitting as the title poem for this, my first poetry book.

That started me coming down without fail on the first Saturday of every month for the open mike.

I quickly got to know those involved and got more involved with the many creative projects available through Cascade Creative recovery. It fitted so well with my creative recovery. Song writing, music and poetry had already started to play a major part of my life, since my recovery from alcoholism and addiction started some 6 years ago. In sobriety I have discovered a self I never knew through artistic means.

I was embarrassed to be called a poet to begin with, but I've learnt if enough people tell me, eventually I start to believe it. I have gained so much from my experience here in Brighton. Initially through Cascade and then Invisible Voices who've kindly invited me to write this book. That has been a particularly inspiring relationship, without even trying, as I spoke to the IV team I seemed inspired to write poems they seemed to like, often about issues they were promoting. Some of those are included in this collection.

I've got more involved here in Brighton, in fact so much so that I decided to move here from London last year. I've had so many opportunities to perform both my poetry and songs on so many positive projects and have performed at both the Brighton Fringe and The Brighton Festival. All those I've met here whether local or DFL's (down from London) like me, are so positive and supportive. It's an easy place to make connections and everybody wants one other to succeed in whatever their endeavours.

I continue to be involved in so many projects:

I will shortly be hosting a second monthly open mike event at Cascade for poetry/spoken word/storytelling/song writing.

The Storytelling Army is set to return next year having just published a book called "Everyday Epic" of all the storytelling we did May '17.

My first Fringe show this year at Venue 101 on May 12th from 2 till 4pm, celebrating IV book launches with music and poetry.

The Washing Up show featuring original songs and poetry, for Brighton Festival on May 19th at Pavilions Richmond house, 20th at Hangleton Community Centre and 26th at Manor Gym.

You'll always find me at the regular Open mikes at Cascade where my journey started.

Big Love Ró

Brighton

The Queen of Brighton

You have a sense of majesty
Now set adrift.
No longer anchored to this island.
On the horizon there's no ship.
Though you are barren
Your decks they are cleared.
Through your twisted remains,
Your memories revered.

Last time we met
Your decks they were filled,
With colourful guests dancing.
Music through the air trilled.
Those who were happy with no country.
Joyful freedom from all rules.
Then you were left in flames.
Now you lie in ruins.

We bow before your beauty
My memory I declare
Your majesties in our hearts
Our love it is sincere

You are the Queen of Brighton.
Though follies and pavilions try
They cannot outshine you.
Our souls now entwine.

With a rusty metal crown
Your beauty I still see
You are The Queen of Brighton
The Queen of the sea.

Another Night Shore

Milky ocean lapping 'gainst the shingle.
On gleaming wet sand the street lights glisten.
They share a table on the grand bandstand.
A breathless melody hangs in the night air.

All is still on this dark moonless night.
A gap in the clouds, distant stars twinkle.
Perseid meteor shower, I'll sit and wait.
The clouds close in, I sit and write.

I see the ghostly outline of the West Pier.
Picked out by city light, a shimmering mirage.
Flashing red warning buoys surround her now.
The bright lights of wind farm mark the horizon.

The dull orange flickers dotted along this shore.
Tucked in by the pier a little fire glows.
Some neon tipped rods where hope springs eternal.
A bright searchlight on a boat seeking.

The melody stops. He's stood up from the table.
She sits, sips the last of their wine.
They look self-conscious stood alone on this stage.
And off they go while the table remains.

I slip away from the shore to anonymous street.
Cars hiss rhythms like unrelenting waves.
A drunk fumbles in his pockets sat on a wall.
As I turn and walk away.

Starlings

Starlings on staves of telephone wire.
No pauses, metre, beats to the bar.
Scattered dots, random melody inspired.
A soft air echoes from afar.

Murmuration on an autumn eve.
Melodies appear before me.
Feel the texture and timbre, tasting
All those flavours fills me.

Words, from silence, form rhythm.
Images fall into rhyme.
Visions graced before me,
I follow the lead, in mind.

Find the path to a quiet head space.
Leave fear, abandon self-doubt.
Allow hands freedom to write.
Words, music and truth will out.

Overwhelmed with thoughts and feelings.
Withheld, stifled for a lifetime.
All wrapped in heartfelt beats,
In Soulful melodies entwined.

Slowly come home to roost
Be still the music of this day.
Writing now complete.
All spiritual debts repaid.

Can't Fool This Night

Brighton town, bright lights of this city.
Crawling around the pavement
On hands and knees.
No one will notice as I shuffle by,
Hidden right in front of you.
Under your nose, but you can't see.
Guess you'd rather not be me
On this path, this night, cold dark light.

You sit in the warm chatter, glowing inside
As the waiter pours your wine.
Piping hot food, I taste through windowless eyes
As I gaze from the dirty side.
Young lives shine, in cosy company entwined.
The warmth, the rich scent of a night well spent
Sweeps by as the café doors flung wide.
I kneel, this night, cold dark light.

And still outside imagining the inside.
My fantasy entwined with your reality.
No escaping my maddening duality.
Am I here, am I there, I'm nowhere

Not even on this ground.
Can't stand to be around my reality
The can in hand my sanity.
I lie, this night, cold dark light.

Always the night that shines through...
I know I can't fool you, 'till daybreak...
When I'm shook awake in the cold morning light...
No I can't, I just can't fool this night.

Invisible Voices & Cascade

Drowned Out Voices, Hidden Choices

Don't see the desolation in their eyes
Their weather beaten skin.
Only see them closed and relaxed
Deep tan and calm within.
Laying in your own detritus
Your blood blackened limbs.
You smelled fresh, looked clean and fit to me.
My denying eyes, my Sin.

On the path of Camden road they sit
Begging for a dollar.
I see them on a beach
At their servants they holler.
In shaky hands a can of Super
Wrapped in a paper bag.
Ragged coats over filthy bare skin.
Drinking cocktails from coconut shells.
Lithe suited bodies waiting for a swim.

The snarling, smoke spewing traffic clogs the road.
The sneering passer-by.
Beautiful tube like sea rollers.

The gulls' plaintive cries.
Tall piss stained street lights
These fellows together don't talk.
The dappled shade of a palm lined path
Upon which my close friends walk.

My deepest desire is to join them
On their carefree life holiday.
So many beaches to choose from
And free cocktails, all day!
It's where my madness takes me
I have no doubt at all.
If I want it take one drink
And eventually there I'll fall.

Saw you laying in Wood Green
Just the other day.
I wanted to lift and hold you,
But I just walked away.
I've pissed myself and slept in doorways
For a night or two.
Even though I had a place to go.
Never truly homeless like you.

I Leap In My Dreams

The weight of my leaden arms,
My heavy legs
Impounded in this embalmed body.
My metal chair, my steel wheeled stallion
I alone can't ride.
I feel so helpless, how do I rediscover my pride.

Abandoned in this ivory tower
I'm placed, but I can't escape.
No space to wheel from room to room.
Even getting to the toilet is beyond me.
The street so far below, a dream, a fantasy.
That I might one day go there, on my own.

How light I'd feel, to be free.
Perhaps to free at last that dancer
That still flails within
Looking to express without.
So much of me aches.
How I rage for what has been taken from me.
How I despair having to fight every inch.

All that I had now lost.
From adult to kid
To growing pains, again!
I want to escape this reality,
This present, this ever present.
I want to sleep, to dream.
To leap and spin, to land
Feel the ground beneath my feet
And once again leap.

Awakened, though saddened
Faced with my reality.
I feel like that physics duality
At once a particle and a wave form
Both solid and light,
Depending on who perceives.
What do you see when you look at me?

A heavy man in a shiny metal chair,
Led lights on my wheels.
Yes I've pimped my ride and who wouldn't.
Can you yet see me.
The head that smiles, the light in my eyes.
Can you see beyond the head tilted
Doughy eyed, simpering smiles.

Afraid to talk to me,
With so many questions in your head.
What happened, how did he get like that.
Was it a crash, a disease,
Is he infectious?
Embarrassed that you might be found out
Your thoughts seized.
And like the rest, you walk away
Unaware you've been staring at me.

I see you, like so many before.
I'm so used to it. Immune?
Not really, just accepting.
That's how people are sometimes.
Now my invisible voice is seen,
In black and white in front of you.
Is heard, loud from the stage.
I hope it leaps from this page or screen.
As I leap, in my dreams.

Walk Alone?

Between a pub and a Buddhist centre
Lies a coffee shop.
The road less travelled by they took.
Smashed windows boarded up.
Graffitied gratitude list
All passer-by's can see.
Maybe more curious made
Might wander in for a chat.
Asking which road they'd take.
Given the choices we inside made
And make again this day.

What treats the sober life may offer.
Which road through the yellow wood
Being the lone traveller to choose,
If they could.
And if not, what then?
Alone to wander, torn asunder
By ravages of drugs and drink.
Would we leave you alone to shirk and shrink
Under the constant pressure?

Come on in and share our pleasure,
If only for a while.
Safe here, warm inside.
Love betides and truth betimes.
And familiar a madness too
For like me like you.
Where else I find such
Solace and comfort but among my own.
Here or out there beyond the reach
Of this simple cafe.

Make of it whatever you please.
Make of us and you might meet your like.
Take a seat, stay a while.
Have you a better place to go?
If you don't take the risk to stay
How would you ever know.
If only an oasis of calm in today's storm
And at that only a brief moment.
Still we are here, as much as we can be.

I have sat in this cafe and sang.
Swapped songs heartfelt and sincere
Of loss, of love, songs of grief,
And happier times, poems too.
Heard armies of storytellers,
Theatre dwellers and all in between.
The cascading voices of the choir sings
Of a freedom that a moment's love brings.

From this moment to another
As we share our journeys together
Wherever they lead.
We all have our choices through the yellow wood.
Many roads, not knowing where they go.
If I should take this or that way.
Who I might meet.
Where I'm going matters not
Only where I am, today.

So together we'll travel.
Maybe for a day or longer.
The road will be shorter with each other.
A journey shoulder to shoulder
We go emboldened by fellows well met
Who travel this path.
By fellows I'll bet
Whose shoes have long travelled.
For it is through those steps
That I go to find my soul.
A journey I can't make on my own.
We don't walk alone!

Recovery

The Searchlight

The searchlight beams through the darkest soul.
Looking for troubles, those troubles of old.
Outwardly seeking anything to find.
Latch onto that its grist to grind.

Grinding, milling, year after year.
Waiting, yearning in the deepest fear.
Alone in the night, no light for the blind,
Can help you see this darkness of mind.

Others would come to rescue you then.
Can't help themselves, beaten men
Caught in shadow plays, gripped, can't see.
Project the knight in shining armour, to thee.

Rescue can't help anyone in this play.
Lost and alone 'till the very day.
When your light beams right in your eyes.
The blindness subsides. The fear dies.

Now the bravest of all can know the truth.
Underneath the surface, right to the root.
Of troubles you know, but never behold,
What lay in the darkness, out in the cold.

In this sight there's a warmth to feel.
Darkness retreats, what remains is real.
Laid out before you, drink in, to fulfil.
Now sated and ready for life to distil.

The Chase

The chase is over, it's hard to let go.
Back and forth I roll, unsure how to show
I care for you. It's not being cruel.
The way things happen is not by rules.
I think it means far more than it does.
To meet my own needs is all I can do.
Hard to trust in the power above,
As it's something I never knew.

To worry and obsess in fear and dread.
Keeps me up, don't seek my bed.
It's harder then to find the space,
For peace of mind, be in the place
Where no problems are too big to solve.
Just given the time to resolve.
The answers are just beyond my grasp.
I hope to get there make it last.

It's all about living on life's terms.
My truth will out, eventually.
My past is hard to face and see.
Fills me with doubt and uncertainty
If not with god then it's harder it seems.
To be on my own, alone, with dreams
And Fantasies of what might be
And who'll take care of you and me.

Midas Miner

Blinded by fear, to the shadows I fled
From this world as my heart bled.
Everyone I've seen is buckled and broken.
What can I do, when love's but a token.

The flaws, injustice, my judgement's true.
Shape it, whittle it, sculpt to my tune.
Straighten it out by will alone.
Forsaking all others, regain control.

The splinters and sparks, as I chip away.
Convinced of the beauty, if I do it my way.
Nuggets of pure gold, my eyes gleam.
Keep hacking, bashing, convinced of this seam.

Never stopping or looking to see what I've done.
Keep trashing forever, driven by some
Infernal engine, fuelled by pure will.
What would happen if I just sit still.

Put these tools down, stop for a while.
Leave this pit, go outside.
My eyes open, a glimpse, a view.
A new dawn, starts to breakthrough.

This Midas miner is done in this mine.
I see my reflection, wipe away the grime.
The more I chase, the further it flees.
Time to grow, away from these dreams.

The Chair

He could have fallen from pages of the Akron bible.
With a moustache that'd make Magnum proud.
Deep southern drawl from the corner of his mouth.
Living the programme aloud.

His chair will capture in hope enrapture
All in this room tonight.
The fellows following in empathy glowing.
He'd surely put the drink to fright.

How could you fail when hearing his tale,
To be lifted from the depths of the ground.
His hopeful journal, his joy eternal,
Shared freely with all around.

Only God could impress with him in service.
A witness to His love profound.
To follow his lead, this planted grown seed.
We could do worse than follow his sound.

Advice not given by his story driven,
What shaped this man tonight?
Strength, love and hope offered freely
Will surely free me and banish fear outright.

My love inferred, to this company preferred,
Lest I go and lose my way.
On the straight and narrow, a bulls eyed arrow.
Staying close, I can't lose, today!

Sometimes

Regardless, whether real or imagined
What happened or may have.
Carries the same emotional weight
In this constant flux state.
Connecting to memories, quiet unseen.
By my silent voice, unspoken.
Only through my hands are seen.
Like my music, broken.

Fragmented parts of what made me.
Scattered glimpses, sideways glances.
Did I really do that, is it true?
The will that held it, now unglued.
Will they see, what'll they say?
Will they like, will they strike?
I've only me to care for,
No longer to blame for.

Sit and learn my process.
Truly discover my roots.
Stay on this road, don't digress.
What I believe is my truth.
Given time it will out.
Slowly revealed, in patience concealed.
Then pain will come.
A companion, a guest unwelcome.

Sometimes in a single line,
Another song condensed.
Such work to reveal it.
Such work to feel it.
Then contained I can relive.
Always looking in the past tense
To ultimately forgive,
What only to me makes sense.
Sometimes.

The Drinking Thinkers Sleep

Wait, I need to have a think.
Off to the pub searching
For that eureka moment in drink.
It's always at the bottom, of the next glass.

Barman another stiff thinkers drink.
While I pursue the soap like thought,
I keep grabbing and grasping
But it won't stay caught.

Slipping and sliding it's so tiring
Barring any other thought.
Barman a defeated thinkers drink
Frowned, puzzled, distraught.

Barman an inflated thinker's dink.
I'm sure, wait what am I meant to think?
Barman what will tinkle peep!
Barman, Barman, Doorman, floormat.

How frustrating, infuriating
I just came to think.
No more bothersome thoughts.
Barman, Barman, I feel sunk.

Why am I out in the cold?
Doorman, Doorman why so bold,
I don't care what you thunk.
Just leave me be, let me in. I'm not Drunk!

Barman, Doorman, floormat, cold path.
Can't think, can't drink, can't sleep, can't walk.
Can hardly talk, falling on this sidewalk.
In the gutter I lie, warm cosy lies.

No I didn't fall, no problem here at all.
Now the darkness falls where I fell.
Who knows what truth there is to tell.
And sleep the drinking thinkers sleep.

CIA

What I did, in silence hid.
Blacked out time and again.
What else could I do to hide from you.
Couldn't face the truth within.
Aloneness prevailed, behaviour replayed
Without any self-care.
Such dangerous choices, drowned out voices.
How could I hope to ever hear.

You give me life, love and guidance,
Despite of my self-destructive will.
I was never open to forgiveness,
Fed by anger, never still.
For then I'd feel deep inside
Something I could never name.
My fear gripped me in darkness
In truth, such awful pain.

For a mother void of love.
A son grieved his shame.
Thought her rejection fuelled
After his love was named.

She was sick beyond belief
A madness gripped her cold.
Every bit as isolated
If her truth could be told.

Now the boy is grown
His mother's long since passed.
That his unrequited love
May find peace at last.
He'll carry the flag for the CIA
For the many who are drowned out still.
Those of us who fill pubs and clubs
Whose lives are run on pure will.

Had so many dark times
When I ended up god knows where.
In blackout rooms, all consumed
In strange embraces, I now despair.
There was a time of happiness
I drank, danced and frolicked.
I am a member of the CIA,
Catholic Irish Alcoholics.

A Year of Firsts

A year of firsts, many new beginnings.
Christmas passed with fewer trimmings.
Life can change so terribly fast.
Just hang in there it'll surely last.
Who could have known such dramatic events
Would unfold or be heaven sent.
Walk hand in hand through your darkest hour.
Awake in light for your love to flower.

All around trying hard to live
With all the changes and forgive,
Everyone for their misdeeds.
In so doing planting seeds.
Whether factual, real or imagined.
Your truth is so believably fashioned.
But once accepted no more denial.
No more will life be a trial.

To those who twist and distort this love.
To fashion, control, impose and shove
Their self-will raging free,
What horrors they impose on thee.

Their imposition has not altered.
Their lack of love truly faulted.
God only knows how to tackle
All those I would have shackled.

They may be imprisoned or befogged.
By hateful angry darkness dogged.
Or in the light they may follow thee
Doing your good will, they may be free.
I do not wish to see them hurting,
Their families around them crumbling.
I pray they release all their pain.
Their families may in your light remain.

Now free to receive what you're given.
No longer by falsehoods or illness driven.
Free to feel so many new emotions.
Free to express our devotion.
Free of all past misdeeds,
Free of shame, free to grieve.
Free of sorrow and depression.
Free to love, free of suppression.

All this freedom so overwhelming.
All this love never ending.
All is given free of price.
All received to entice
Some humility and a simple plan.
Like many, sought to understand
And help us see and keep revealing
The purest love our deepest feeling.

Standing Together

Got nothing out of North London
Got nothing out of you.
I'm away to find my own people
Between here and Timbuktu.
Things are so much better
Chelsea's free of hoi polloi.
Famous people hereabouts,
Make me a happy boy.

Had enough of herself at home
My kids can lump it too.
I'm away to Kensington now
Where my people are so true.
Christian, Ben and Bartholomew
Know what I'm all about.
Better than any round here,
Of that I have no doubt.

And if not there then elsewhere
I'm sure to search them out.
The rich, the famous are fallen
They're waiting, it's my shout!

Ahoy lads I'm here now,
Hope you've not waited long
This trips my disaster recovery.
Sing my geographical song.

I've felt just as powerless
Then I feel myself abuse.
Any and all about me
All kindness refused.
A frightening reminder
Of a madness, just like mine.
Want to believe it's further away
But like you it's a day at a time.

Then when I reveal
Some deep and darkened secret.
Discovered with my silent voice
I feel so scared and decrepit.
I sit there uncomfortably
With my truth stripped bare
I run away to cover up
The shame, the guilt, the long stare.

When we became friends
Spending time together.
You helped me be more vulnerable
Sharing our songs, our banter.
I allow and quickly forgive,
What I wouldn't from others.
When fellowship becomes
Standing together as brothers.

The Floodwaters

The flood waters are receding
The tide ebbs.
No longer am I bleeding
The tears wept.
Eyes sore from crying,
My throat dry.
No longer wondering,
I can see why.

How I am with my fellows
And with my friends.
There's work to be done
Truly make amends.
Repair the damage
My tongue has done.
Not the words said
It's the feelings that stung.

It rises deep down
When I'm reflected
In another's story.
I get distracted

My hackles rise
It leaps from my tongue
I chastise,
Then damage is done.

Not the 39 steps
Or the 10 commandments,
The seven deadly sins
By which I'm reprimanded.
Not 3 steps to heaven
Nor a 2 step country dance.
But another set of steps
Which give me a chance.

Embracing all humility
I can gather inside.
Suppressing my will,
Deflating my pride.
They've only been distractions
Purely self-serving.
Denying all those who were
Always more deserving.

The respect I didn't give
To all, I suppose.
Too stubborn to forgive
In my denials repose.
Disconnected, unfeeling
Always sought to shove
My truth, I couldn't share
With those I couldn't love.

I was in such pain
From childhood till that day.
When I awakened
To the debts I had yet to pay.
Slowly guided on this path,
Some days even carried
As journeys end and start.
To my trust and faith married.

Relationships

Silence Sale

You bought my silence with your tears.
I sold my silence for your pain.
Happiness is nowhere to be seen.
We need to find ourselves again.

You bought my silence with reversal.
I sold my mine with persistence.
Don't say what we need to
Can't stop this expanding distance.

You bought my silence with your fears.
I sold my silence for your assurance.
Got all mixed up without tears.
Time to face this with endurance.

You bought my silence with your blame.
I sold mine without concern.
Don't want to face our shame.
Now I think it's time to learn.

Time to stop the silence sale.
Time to look and see what's there.
Underneath so many veils.
What we find we can share.

In your silence perhaps to soothe.
In my silence I face my grief.
Time to look to our own truth
And go forward with belief.

You bought my silence with your rage.
I sold mine for dreadful fear.
Trying to find another page
For my words, my voice to hear.

We trade our silence all these years.
I try to make my heart declare,
Never revealed, kept secret layers.
What good is love, if it's not shared?

Brother

I long for the brother I never had.
I mourn his passing. I miss him so.
Overwhelming yearning, my feeling sad
Who is he, will I ever know?
I have no picture of his face
In my mind's eye.
No reference to his embrace.
But dear god, I miss him so.

My fantasy history gone.
Stripped bare, I shiver.
I never knew me,
Nor would I let myself be known.
He knew me. He loved me.
He held me in his arms.
The love my brother gave
Is like no other.

Together, we conquer all.
With you beside me, I have no fear.
We are there for each other
Should we fall from grace or shame of face
No judgement will come to bear.
We shall simply be,
With each other, there to share
Whatever has been, or will be.

Body Commodity

All I am is a body commodity.
How can I ever love
Never having received it freely
How can I be free of these chains,
My shattered remains
Fallen in this barren room,
Eyes pleading, feeling ashamed.

What they took then, they take again.
Like yesterday, and every day.
The price I pay for all their sins.
I don't pay it alone for I have sinned
All I have spent, all I ever had.
Running forever without a plan.
No one else, really, gives a damn.

All I've ever known is what I've done.
And what's been done to me.
I am chained to this fool, knowing one rule.
You will never know love,
here or above while will runs free.

And what I've craved, became depraved.
I thought it could be bought.
I'll meet your needs,
But no deal can ever be sealed, if love is to be real.

How can I give away what's never been given?
How can I feel what I've never known?
How can I do what's never been shown?
It's impossible, alone.

Forged In The Past

We lived in a friendship forged in the past.
And every time we'd meet
We'd talk about the last time.
The last time, we did the same.
Did we ever have a past?
Or just imagined that we were friends
Or thought we should be
Simply because of the passage of time.

And drink. Oh how we'd drink,
And then another sup.
And fight. Oh how we'd fight
And then make up.

And gone, until we happened to meet again.
Weeks, months, even years passed.
Your absence, unnoticed.
So close were we, really?
And how when we met
So sad to have our absent friendship.
Again to regale, relive, some lost feeling
Some lost connection to ourselves.

And drink. Oh how we'd drink,
And then another sup.
And fight. Oh how we'd fight
And then make up.

We grieved together our lost mothers.
So sad, we'd see through each other's eyes
Those that didn't, those of us that daren't cry.
Too afraid to admit, we were on our own.
Rejected, abandoned, set adrift
And on the horizon, no ship.
Though on Dublin's foggy nights
We'd hear them call.

To Skulk Away

To skulk away behind a song
That says the words you won't say.
I was closer to you than you to me.
The last song I sent you, my tears lent you.
To never say the friendship's over.
Never say why you've gone.
Never say you no longer belong.
Never write together, another song.

I'm angry, depressed, bargaining any test.
To see how to remain, together in song.
That's not easy to sit with, the never known.
The whys, the wherefores, I'll never know.
What is it, that reflection, of you on me.
What is it, the pain between us.
What is it that separates us.
Fear came and stopped me.

Next time I'll stay with friends who accept me.
No matter who I am, and who I am is free.
And you are free from whatever it is.
And you can see whoever you are.
What lies in you beyond the fear.
What lies behind your secret tears.
The never-known, the never-shown.
In shadows where my truth lay.

In silent shadows you can't say.
But you can, you must, you will.
Whenever your time comes
Then you'll say, and it'll be ok.
Don't forget to shout
Loud enough for me to hear.
And rest assured I'll be there
When your truth will out.

And slowly the fear goes and we are free.

Free My Broken Family

Free my broken family.
Live apart in peace.
Free myself from enabling,
The cost of my disease.
Had to feel needed
To show I really care.
Had to feel heeded
To feel loved, not despair.

The roads mapped out before me.
I know it's proper and right.
Having worked for many years,
Prayed, seen the light.
Still so hard and painful
Letting go of all control.
Still so dreadfully fearful
Of my talents to show.

What if I'm successful,
I get what I want.
I feel so undeserving
Having served others wants.

I put myself down so low
My needs don't matter.
Pummel myself to ground
My own worth I shatter.

All that I value,
All I want to share
All the gifts you give me
Truly belong out there.
Serve your will, I must.
Turn mine to dust.
Sometimes easier said than done
Some days so hard to trust.

My heads full of lies
Can't sleep through the night
Of all my past misdeeds
Can't feel the pain that's right here now
Where I don't want to stay.
How will I ever tell my kids
I'm about to move away.

Let Them Go

The hardest place of all to bring
Over the threshold into my home.
I cannot shirk, I cannot silence,
When my truth is finally known.

Although I doubt I cannot alter.
The fear is so very real.
Now I've started I cannot stop.
For true love there is no deal.

With serene intent, honest heart
Can't avoid hurting those I love.
Put aside anger make a start.
There'll always be a family to love.

The bravest will be given courage.
The truest love of all to know.
On this path you cannot falter.
Face your truth and "Let them go!"

Music

King of Pipers

At 12 years of age I sat there listening to him play
At the Willie Clancy festival
Down in Milltown Malbay
Camping in Spanish Point
For a week without a care
For anything but the music
That's where my passion declared.

Me Dad brought me there
With me pipes in hand to learn.
Listening to pipers play
In pubs 'till break of dawn.
Walking back to the campsite
Myself and dad alone.
Talking of tunes and pipers
All the way back home.

Then off to a concertina show,
Never heard their likes before.
Then a hush descended,
We were gripped from door to door.
He came out upon on the stage
With a smile upon his face.

Telling stories, playing tunes,
Lifted the roof off the place

I sat there enraptured
It's still with me now.
As he sat there explaining
The "Talk" and "Truckley Howl".
He could wrap his fingers
Round the chanter
At least two times or more
And play the melody
Like no one else before.

With elbow on the bellows,
Arm upon the bag.
The pipes began to breathe,
The drones began to brag.
A tune leapt from the chanter.
Oh how my heart did soar.
The eminent Seamus Ennis
We'll hear his likes no more.

Spiritual Treason

Take flight through the upper registers.
Plunge to whip along the grass tops.
A guttural response, atonal, arrhythmical.
Grieving's rise to a crescendo.
The birds themselves, small and quiet.
A subtle chord on an octet of strings
Slowly changing shape, shifting colour
Over the long passage of time 'till nightfall.

When the shadows rise and silence falls
And another movement calls.
Clusters of quickly played piano notes.
Another chord rises, deep in the near distance.
Bass tones swirl below, rising and falling
Dip my wings in their crests as I fly.
A brittle scratching so high and rough textured.
No sooner perceived then gone.

They argue and cackle, what a row.
Now they come together
Woodwind, breathy, wet,
These voices this night.

The clarinet speaks above
The oboe's long cycled notes.
And all falls against the long forgotten chord.
It was there since the beginning.
Now greeted like an old friend.

In sure embrace held aloft
In this reign of notes.
Melodies long since parted.
Quieted now life's rhythms sung.
There is rhyme in death
Griefs waves corrode reason.
Crashing cymbals, timpanists drum.
In furious grey seas, my spiritual treason.

Night Song

The single line, a thought in time.
As we sat on steps, your song caressed the night.
Of a love you sang, a lone voice in flight.
Softly played strings reveal heartfelt beauty
No longer concealed.
Who is it that adorns the air.
In this moment I am immersed in your song.
You have another powerful singer.
But deep in your soul such beauty lingers

I can hardly remember words that have hung
For so very long since they were sung.
Who is this man this Midas miner
Arising from the pits makes the night brighter.
The cold night air was warmed
As your melody swam and swirled.
Round your words, your voice unfurled.

The rising waters lifted us, we were afloat.
The minutes of your song lasted longer
And still linger.
I heard you sing before,

Even though I've known you
I met a new you that night.
Is your song still in flight?

Could it be you standing alone
With your guitar
Surrounded by stars?
Please reveal who you are.
Let them all see and hear
What you have to share.
The love from brother to brother
Is like no other.

Glyndebourne to Brighton

The girls get their opinions off their chest.
Boys playing clackers on the coast.
While over the sleepers memories jostle
On this train from Glyndebourne to Brighton

No longer hammering on piano keys
Playing atonal sounds of childhood tragedy
The baby grand and I sang.
Or plucking the uprights harp-like strings.
Having sat, numb cheeked and listened.
All those arias, anger bristles.
Returned to my home of rehearsals.
A child audience to unwanted guests.

Music and words of my choice.
Ignore the internal infernal voice.
Shoe staring, crippling self-doubt
It bubbles it boils, "I must let it out."
No you're not good enough a composer,
Nor libretto'ist, nor musician.
You can't do it without being studious.
You're nowhere near enough serious.

Such conflict, I wanted to be you.
She called me by your name.
I simply couldn't follow you
I forgot to be me.
Blinded by my own stupidity
Or maybe just a child that couldn't see.
Again reborn from eternal death
From the bowels of Mother Earth.

The umbilical threads dangle.
In long chords entangled,
But I do not feel ensnared.
She's not here, she's no longer there.
The vertical shift, horizontal hold.
The yen to say what lies untold.
Let it dance on my tongue, leap from my dreams.
Let it shine, let it bleed, let it beam.

While the girls get their opinions off their chest.
Boys playing clackers on the coast.
While over the sleepers memories jostle
On this train from Glyndebourne to Brighton.

Spirituality

Little G

To find you I've returned to when I was a child.
Speaking to a friend, in my garden for a while.
No one knew this imaginary friend of mine.
Held my hand, walked me, as we talked for a time.
When asked I said "The Poke", I know what I meant.
You were there to help, I talked it made sense.
I can't see who it was, the presence I felt then.
Now I recall you, find my beginning, again.

Chose to be without, I wallowed in the abyss.
A struggle I didn't need
Through your love I'll find bliss.
Have no race, creed or colour I can see.
No sex distinction or look like you and me.
All to me as I walk with you,
Been given many names.
Care not how I ask, you'll answer just the same.
Though I've been a stranger, that I will admit.
You will care for all, to your knowing I submit.

Many years have passed, many lives I've led.
Felt you close, but unaware of you instead
Busy doing this and that, not ready to see.
Who I am, what it's like, truly being me.
Little g is the piece of god energy I found.
Like gravity helped keep my feet on the ground.
Whether I knew it or not
You were there for my needs.
On my terms you met me. You planted a seed.

I humbly surrender to my god above
All that I am and all that I love.
Find peace in myself, love that is true.
I submit all of me in trust and love to you.

Let God Guide Me

Affairs of the head
That make my mind race.
Slow those thoughts,
Lead me to a serene place.

Refrain:
Let god guide me.
Be grounded,
Feel centred,
By love surrounded.

Affairs of the heart
That thump through my chest.
Still that beast
Allow my body to rest.

Refrain:
 Let god guide me.
Be grounded,
Feel centred,
By love surrounded.

Affairs of the body
Illness, aches and pains.
To all who ask.
All ailments relieved.

Refrain:
Let god guide me.
Be grounded,
Feel centred,
By love surrounded.

Affairs of the soul,
Those deep troubles of old.
Allow love to heal
And all truths will unfold.

Between Me and You

There were so many, now so few.
These gods between me and you.
I needed them then not so today.
They clutter my view being in the way.
They were there when I sought them,
To light my way. Not alone on my darkest days.
Now I see them in my mind's eye,
Shining light on the past from which I shy.

They are my voice, they are my muse.
That I face my truth no longer confused.
They guide me to you my path is clear.
That I may stand tall knowing you are near.
I've spiritually shifted. I don't walk alone.
Seeing today what I never could've known.
Through my pain you walk with me,
Meeting the needs I can't see.

I call on you kneel and pray,
That I may live in amends today.
Now standing tall in your expanse.
On this stage how shall I dance.
Or would I sing or recite my poems.
All those words to me you've loaned.
The melodies and notes played.
Phrases, rhymes and rhythms tried.

All an invitation to be real.
Triggered by empathy, permission to feel.
And share your truth we don't stand alone.
We listen and hear as we each atone.
There is no judgement, full quarter given.
This is our stage share your truest vision.
Set fear aside express your love, hopes and dreams.
Share with us your truth. That we may all heal.

My Higher Power and Me

My Higher Power is my father.
My Higher Power is my mother.
For those named and their like
We walk together as brothers.

My Higher Power is my conduit,
My direct line to God.
My Higher Power is Love.
May I receive what I had not.

My Higher Power is a poet.
My Higher Power Sings.
All these words and music,
My inspiration brings.

My Higher Power has laughter
Sadness, joy and tears.
Many feelings in between,
My learning will take years.

My Higher Power guides me.
However I may ask.
My Higher Power carries me,
Through the growing pains tasked.

My Higher Power was waiting
The days that I died.
My Higher Power forgives
All those that lied.

My Higher Power is with me
Every moment of my life.
My Higher Power guides me,
Through my troubles and my strife.

My Higher Power waits
In serenity and peace.
My Higher Powers allows me
To face all my grief.

My Higher Power stands
Big and powerful above all.
My Higher Powers protects
That I may never again fall.

My Higher Power gives love
Fed by God above.
That I may have this moment.
To learn and spread His love.

Love Everlasts

My Freeze, a tabernacle
My fight for rebirth.
My Inner Critic, the stick
To beat myself to death.

My Fears a rod
From throat to crotch.
My Flight the bones
On my back latched.

My Rage all swollen.
My stomach bulged.
Self-Righteous anger
Never divulged.

My Submission deep
Weighs down my core.
Out of my mouth
For You to adore.

On my hands and knees
It's you I beseech.
Once again I call.
My troubles deep.

I feel sunk far below
No waves above.
Brought to Your house
Await Your love.

And work and ask
What would you have me do.
Connect to myself
Bid my troubles adieu.

In Your care
My life's recast.
In Your light
Love everlasts.

Politics

Suicide Nation

Parents, teachers, priests, politicians.
They all let us down no sign of contrition.
Their silence, as deafening, as our isolation.
Can't speak up, we're the lost generation.
Feeling fenced in, the bird in a cage.
Trying to find our voice, let out our rage.
Constrained by rules, Government regulation.
Can't speak up, we're the lost generation.

They have to be seen to impose the rules.
Single us out, an example for fools.
Our futile attempt to get attention.
Can't speak up, we're the lost generation.
If we fight all the time, we'll never win.
Choose our battles, don't give in.
Allow them to help, affirmative action.
Can speak up for our lost generation.

Think they should, have to, or must.
These are our rules, turn them to dust.
Can't impose our love revolution
If we want to leave our lost generation.
Change doesn't happen straight away.

Give all a chance and change our way.
Speak together tuned to the same station.
Leave in memory, our lost generation.

No more will we project our blame.
Time to realise our silent shame.
No more a call of Murderation!
Time to end our suicide nation.

Sold Out Nation

Livin' since the great recession.
Who cares for the minor silent majority.
Their political lies leave a bad impression.
Greed, is the drug, their priority.
We don't even bother to vote these days.
We feel the loss, we feel the pain
Unsure why this is happening today?
They've sold our future, for their own gain!

To bankers, shareholders, blue bloods too.
We let them get away with the crime of the century.
Golden parachutes given to the few,
Who failed us so miserably, left us in slavery.
To billions in bailouts and quantitative easing.
Printing cash like it's going out of fashion.
Their bulging bank balance, greed, self-pleasing.
We foot the bill for their money passion.

We're heading back to the 50's and before.
Can't afford a degree or get a job in Mc Donald's.
Live in poverty forever-more.
While the rich get richer, line their pockets.
They've made a money grab there's no doubt.

The growing chasm between rich and poor.
They laugh and take the food from our mouths.
They're in plain view not behind closed doors.

Disenfranchised, abandoned, ignored.
We let them away with it truth be told.
Their arrogance should be deplored.
The reality of having our future sold.
For all our lives our children's too.
We're indentured, enjoy your libation.
To hell with us all for the benefit of you.
Look what you've done, "Sold out our Nation!"

Take The Queen's Shilling

A city of nervous wrecks, I'd have thought.
Streets paved with PTSD the troubles brought.
Bullet by bullet, bomb by bomb.
Singing wrap the flag round me,
Or some other song.
Street by street, home by home.
No family escapes this thunder dome.
Brothers, Sisters, torn limb from limb.
There's no reason enough to kill our kin.

A hail of bullets from a child with gun.
A head full of resentments
Passed from father to son,
Mother to daughter, generations weeping.
What now, we've left our children sleeping.
Never will they awake to play without end.
These silent empty streets have no friends.
Look around, there's nothing left
But the echoes of war as the gun-smoke lifts.

Kill any old tourist and their sons
Mothers, children or anyone.
How did their deaths further your cause?
Another friendly fire incident, your riposte.
Stolen one by one, breath by breath.
Was it worth it? All this death!
Earned your right at the tables of those you fought.
Your ticket like the rest,
By the blood of others bought

And you survived, generals of war.
Made your blood money where's your encore.
The political kudos, brave peacemakers.
Empty words from double dealing fakers.
Where will it end your paths soiled with souls
Of many young who'll now never grow old.
Let's forget the killing as the traitor sits.
Take the Queen's shilling if the suit fits.

Oh Lordy Gratitude Boardy

If honesty is the first chapter in the book of wisdom.
And a rebellious act in a time of deceit.
Feed the rebellion with your truth,
Deafen their lies, let reality speak.
The lies may win some battles.
Don't be silent, despair nor sabre rattle.
By peaceful means let no blood be spilt.
Passive resistance going full tilt.

We have the power to no longer consume.
The poor shareholders, profits gloom.
Hit them in the pocket stay free of debt.
That's why we've no freedom left.
Each new loan creates the money.
Indentured slaves smell the honey.
Quick buy it now before it's too late
You'll be a long time dead, greed to sate.

How are we to protect our young.
Allow their small songs to be sung.
It makes no sense, I can't relate.
You must be indebted to educate.

Our political leaders have lost the plot.
Sunk deep in the pockets of the banker's pot.
And how they reward the wealthy and greedy
Each new week creates many more needy.

It's no wonder our streets fill and overflow
With the dumped, expelled human cargo.
How it rankles, uneasy guilt,
Rolling in their own filth.
Yes you! With your filthy lucre stashed.
Care not a jot for those you've dashed
So hard against the paving slabs.
Dose the pain in your hearts not stab?

How much do you need to stash away.
Did it rain on St Swithuns day.
What use will money be to you then?
Won't get you through the gates of heaven.
But see you all the way to hell.
For your truth, so afraid to tell
Stop it now before it's too late
Qualify for a full love rebate.

Through this love you'll surely profit.
The richest of all men find their prophet.
To be disgorged of ill-gotten wealth.
So unburdened your freedom felt.
The gap in your soul will melt away.
Now sated this and every day.
This alone will see you through.
Ask only your gods will for you.

Trauma

Changeling

Can't see their faces, don't know their names.
Behind my mask lies my shame.
Their black eyes look, but they can't see.
I long for them, do they love me?
I do what I'm told, I'm a good boy.
They give me a drink, I'm their toy
I think they care, they're so engaging,
Laugh and charm, my young changeling.

Big blue eyes, blond curls, sallow skinned,
Eye catching child. I was saddened,
When your abuse of me was done.
I couldn't speak up, I was too young
I'm older now, though thoughts are dim
I speak in a way I never did.
My truth will out, won't protect your sin,
The cost of our shame, for that I condemn.

To death! I place the power of our memories
You were there too, what of your identities?
They will out, how far I don't know.
The cost for you, a damn I'll not show!
You stole my heart, shattered my soul.
Took away my safety, destroyed my home.
Did what you liked, sated your desires.
Cheated, drugged, an innocent in your arms.

Then I grow, shattered, broken.
Never knew true love, it's only a token.
Never felt safe or secure anywhere
All these escapes and fantasies shared.
Never at peace, unable to trust,
The damage you caused, truly unjust.
You will pay, for all that you've done.
You stole my childhood, just for fun!

Fragile Smile

Through the crazed veneer of my fragile smile.
The tears seep from the depths of time.
Brush it off, brave it out. Let no one see
Wear the mask of denial, as belligerent be.

In the playground they wait.
Under cover in the shade, over by the gate.
What if they ask "You're late, why?"
What will I say to continue the lie?

Just got away, stop! Look around, it's okay.
Lean back 'gainst the white wall,
Remember, don't say!
Stiffen up, stand straight,
Shake that look off my face.
They will not know today, of my disgrace.

Exhale, out, in again, breathe shivers,
From the base of my spine to my shoulders,
Fear quivers.
What happened today lies buried stranded
On how many others was this fear branded.

Shame face instead of my fragile smile,
A look in my eyes, again today my childhood dies.
No one knows what's hidden, all these years
Least of all me, only cried secret tears.

This boy doesn't cry, no wonder.
A silent quake, inner thunder.
Outside all's quiet, calm.
Inside the fury breaks through the dam.

I'm Compelled

Given freedom to do as I'm compelled.
No longer so selfishly propelled
By all the distractions in this world.
As I connect to myself, my life's unfurled.
It doesn't matter how I dress.
Whose embrace, or who I caress.
We have our own moral code.
No one tells us "Do what you're told."

First to grieve then forgive all those
Who've wronged me through the throws
Of unspeakable acts, so cruel and violent.
From early years through teenage silence.
And on through drug addled adulthood.
I feared to face, my will withstood
And held back all my painful truths.
'til I relented, released the roots.

Then came the time, I heard the call.
To hand over my will, before I fall.
My choice surrendered, courage earned,
My trust restored, memories returned.
Of all I carried, alone each day.
A burden too big, the price I paid.
And those close to me suffered too
As I would not to myself be true.

If I digress, the pain I'll feel
And on others I'll impale.
To sit with it, then I'll know.
If in doubt to pray will show
The way of things and how to be
Not spinning blindly, then we'll see.
What all this love will surely bring.
For my praise I write and sing.

Faith Never Shaken

My left hand shakes uncontrollably
From my little finger to my middle.
Like you were pulled out of me
I feel numb and lost in this riddle
You came from under my chest
There's a gaping hole under my arm
For you I kept close to my breast
To guard you from all harm.

Your head rests here and along my arm
Your tiny body lies.
I look at your withered remains,
You're a part of me that died.
I saw the doctor remove the shreds
From between your mother's legs.
The blood stained floor, never meant to see.
The doctor looks at your dregs.

I've held on to you so long
Many years have passed since the day you died
Now I choose to remember your song.
The tears I owe have yet to be cried.

Feels like threads and sinews of mine
That are being pulled from my body.
I feel it along the length of my arms
The pain unbearably heavy.

Like Dara who went before you
From another mother.
For my failure, I now acknowledge
Him completely as my brother.
For you, my son that couldn't live
Michael Arthur Bodley.
For all my love I couldn't give
I now give to others freely.

To put right my spiritual wrongs
My confused trails hard to follow
A life led in disarray
With a truth so hard to swallow.
Can doubt no more what is revealed.
My right to choose gladly taken.
How else can courage be received.
My faith never again shaken.

Musk Scented Blues

Luxuriated in a denial
I can ill afford.
In the warm unctuous pools.
No bridge to ford
The dark oily slick
Of my self piteous ooze.
In there to wallow
In musk scented blues

Slipping, sliding
Soulless isolation.
Writhing, withering,
Bottomless desolation.
On pale white flesh
Black as pitch glistens.
Hands spreading, squelching
Any truthful emissions.

In this naked repose
Intimate blissful arousal.
No sexual crescendo
Only thoughts of reprisal.

No fear or anger,
Smothered feelings denied.
As they bubble and boil
Lord of all, I preside.

And from the depths,
My Dead Sea scrolls.
Unfurled now reading
The names on my roles
And of all their misdeeds.
Judge, jury and prosecutor
I plan their demise,
Torturous executioner.

And oh, how they'll bleed
In sorrowful admission.
And oh, how they'll plead
To my death-full expression.
For there is no parole,
Never remission.
Only revenge to extol,
Forever imprison.

Then slip from this place,
Fearful reality beckons.
This terrified boy's
Fantasized regressions.
Never speaking or telling
Of their dreadful transgressions.
Colluding for survival.
The cost, my depression.

And oh, how I paid,
Self-medicated my pain.
Addled and confused
Feared they'd come again
And do unto me
What they'd always done.
Another terrifying death
Would I find my sun?

Now my fear recedes
As my truths are seen.
I hear my voice
As I come clean

And tell again
What I've always known.
Free from the shame
Which they've thrown.

And in that shroud
My head hung low.
It pulled me down
My truth, unknown.
Such a heavy burden
Through life I shuffled.
Released by this moment
No longer so troubled.

Now I hear My Soul Sing

You've sat and waited this life long
Ensnared, floored, done no wrong
Hummed and shook nowhere to belong.
Now I see what went wrong.
You waited so well
You're a good little boy
In that room alone no toys.
Lit by morning light as I open the door
You're sat in front of me
Right there on the floor.

You turn and look up, you know me.
Your eyes light up before me.
We share a smile knowingly.
Lifting your arms reaching.
No longer lie beseeching.
Knowing all truths, lies fleeing
Away from those big blue eyes.
Black marks under belie.

The secrets, hidden by others.
How you were torn asunder
A life fragmented, dismembered
Over the years lie scattered
A boy beaten and battered
Used, abused, left confused.
Doused those flames
With the same liquid fuel.
You were nobody's fool
Just dealt a hand so cruel.

Now we embrace, no smiles or disgrace.
I forgive you, you made no mistake.
I thank you for lying awake for me.
You've waited so long and never gave up on me.
Knowing someday I'd come, for me.
Your shard of memory to complete me.
Your loving embrace to remind me.
Such an important message you've carried for me.
Such acceptance and patience you teach me.

A lone light in the darkness you've held aloft for me.
A lone light through the darkness to guide me.
A lone light that flickered so far from me.
A light together we now share
Our embrace completes, repairs
The chasm between my truth and lies.
It has now vanished right before our eyes.

How simple a thing this loving embrace now brings.
How freeing the gift of forgiveness brings.
How peaceful mere patience brings.
How connected and flowing, trust brings.
How all healing pure love brings.
Now I hear my soul sing.

Friends

To Undress the Knight
by Jovannah Bär

The inside of my head is filled
With clouds, instead of brains.
Confusion is running through my veins,
I am so tired.

These dreams are more vivid than ever before
I cannot reassure myself anymore.
Is it my wrong, do you condemn me
For the crazy way I'm wired?

And so I'm counting the dots on your dress,
For a moment I feel a little bit less,
Please, don't look at me,
Let me be part of the background.

Don't you let me unfold,
I'll lose grip of the shield that I hold.
And there's no time in your schedule,
To pick up my pieces off the ground.

I don't know how much of me you can take,
Don't want you to think I was born a mistake.
Is something terrible happening when
I lose it, and end up crying again?

And so I spend every minute around you,
Hiding what's happening , the things that I do.
For I would rather pretend to be okay,
Than to risk driving you away.

To Govern

by Jovannah Bär

Sounds were being absorbed
By the clouds who were patiently waiting
To join the new-borns on their journey
As the politicians were debating,
Nearly fighting over the budgets.
Could money not better be spent,
On pursuing the war in some faraway country,
To raise the status of their own land?

While the real images were being repressed,
From the conscience of the decision-maker.
Making it harder and harder to reign in compassion,
Since the academic is never a convicted law-breaker.
I heard the whispers saying they'll take over
The minds of the opportunistic youth.
And I'm starting to see this power trip,
Based on a series of twisted truths.

While there is a long line of children,
Looking for a sound place to sleep.
Why is the strength of our combined forces,
After centuries still falling into the deep?
Do they really see sense in this strategy?
I will not ever forget the sound of a tortured scream.
Why are those who are supposed to protect us,
Treating history like some long lost dream?

The Night Walk
by Nils Nisse Visser

Well met in midnight's moonlight
Child bruised but unbroken yet.
Your silver laughter breaks the night,
Both real and that of melancholy set
In your mind by another's blind rage.
Yet, despite that dreadful fright,
Despite time spent in a mental cage,
You find the strength to smile so bright.
Half of it acted, half of it real
With sadness in your eyes still
That tells me how you really feel,
Though it's with genuine good will,
That you give me an Elfin treasure
The nearing dawn's first drop of dew
Filling me with delighted pleasure
Baring the golden goodness that is you.

Siren of the Sea
by Nils Nisse Visser

Child of the Ocean, young Siren of the Sea,
Knee-deep in the surf, still as a rock you stand
Overlooking the vastness, your back to me,
Loneliness ahead, behind you the land.
Hand in hand we stand, like soldiers in the ranks,
Now's the moment, the magic flows fast and strong:
Fire in the sky, water, breeze and bare sand banks.
All is whole, so whole, here and now we belong.
Mermaids in the surf, sand, shells, briny spray.
Seize joy, seize love, seize life, fight now to be free,
Like a child splash, dive, swim, in the blue sea play,
Like Ocean's child, like a Siren of the Sea.

Darkness and light
by Robert Powell

Today the sun doesn't shine,
The mood is darker now
The clouds are darkest grey,
But I must not let that show
The darkness is simply
Just a lack of lightness present
It is the dimming down of bright
And sparkling effervescent
But do I need my eyes to see
The rays of the mighty sun
Glinting and reflecting,
Supplying power so I may feel at one
Or can I just imagine,
The darkness is self-imposed
In fact all of its accompaniment
Is simply presupposed
That if it was not for my production,
It'll not be there to find
I made it, I called it, it was a creation
Within my mind
Because something happened,

That made me feel quite bad
But when I gave entry to the darkness
I really felt most sad
I often invite it in
To spend with me some time
As we interlock and bind as partners in a crime
Why did no one tell me
The darkness is not my friend
Why did I not realise,
In its presence,
Time I mustn't spend
That what I really needed,
Was to be guided by my sight
Ignoring all the darkness
So that I may appreciate the light

To Vieri
by Robert Powell

My socks feel wet water seeps in
The endless drops tapping on tin
England's weather, does it always rain?
Why on earth did I not move to Spain?
Perhaps the damp, the wet, the cold
Is what helps me remember as I grow old
That life isn't always a bask in the sun
Life is sometimes, in fact often, not fun
The challenge I find is to not get down
Or fall in a puddle and best not to drown
To establish that water is required for life
And a little wetness is really not strife
If we triumph in weather as it drips and does pour
Then when it improves, we may thrive as we soar
It is a state of weather perceived by the mind
If we lived in a desert then we would see it as kind
That god was delivering a much needed prayer
And that as is in life it can be seen quite fair.

If I was your King
by Robin Patrick Munro Runciman

If I was your King
I'd burn all the money
I'd fill up your dreams
With milk and honey
I'd give back the land
The Lord made for you
To help you understand
An Eden that's true

If I was your King
I'd turn politicians
Into poets of peace
And loving musicians
Away from these prisons
With their visions of division
And back to peace and wisdom
On the love beach of freedom

If I was your King
I'd charge you no fee
Because everything for you
Was meant to be free

I'd build you all homes
Of touchstone and gold
And show you the jewels
Inside of your soul

If I was your King
I'd burn all your greed
By giving you everything
That you could ever need
There's always plenty
When we empty our hands
Try to understand
The true fellowship of man

If I was your King
I'd turn robotic regimes
Into cosmic streams
Full of rock n roll dreams
With a love revolution
Full of musical powers
And a true love solution
Full of beautiful flowers

If I was your King
I'd bring you water from springs
Away from these waters

Polluting your dreams
I'd show you God's Will
With natural health
So you never need to kill
To realise your wealth

If I was your King
I'd show you what's true
I'd show you the miracle
That's eternally you
I'd give you the keys
To help you to see
A Universe that's free
From material disease

If I was your King
I'd give you new wings to fly
Back to Vrndavan
In the Spiritual Sky
'Cause that is the Garden
Where nobody cries
Where nobody lies
And where nobody dies

I Saw a Saintly Vaisnava
by Robin Patrick Munro Runciman

I walked ten thousand deserts
In search of a golden beach
I swam the oceans deepest
For mermaids out of reach
I climbed ten thousand mountains
To kiss the Purple Sky
And I cried ten thousand fountains
For a world that couldn't cry

I heard a lonely poet
Repeat his treasured line
Saying it's only Radha and Krishna
Who give pleasure to mankind
I listened to his world of words
Where troubadours are kings
Inside the Rainbow Universe
Where the blue belle angel sings

I walked the diamond highways
To test my broken feet
To lead me to those skyways
Where Earth and Eden meet

I saw a Cosmic Ferryman
On his purple swan
Flying back home to the fairyland
Beyond the lotus pond

I saw some tongues of politicians
Crippled inside their heads
And some ministers of freedom
Who had hung their hearts instead
I saw a billion battlefields
Where only greed was won
I saw young children in a field
Of graveyards in the sun

I'm a universal beggar
Out here in the cold
Begging the Lord for mercy
To come and free my soul
I've lived through every age
On a plane that's full of change
My body is my cage
And my karma is my chain

I saw a Saintly Vaisnava
On the shores of the Causal Ocean
Saying he'd carry me home to Vrndavan
If I could spare just one tear of devotion
He said each universe was a grain of sand
On the love beach of creation
That each universe was made for man
To reach his final destination

Broken Britain
by Jules Deason

In broken Britain did you eat today?
In Broken Britain where did you sleep today?
Did you have a smile come your way?
Who did you even speak to today?

Were you ignored for what you said today,
Or judged in a merciless way?
Did you share time with a friend today?
Or did your paths not cross, they're out of your way.

Could you afford your bills today?
Were your lifetime's belongings taken away?
Did you get a chance to say all you could,
With no time to delay?

Did you honestly listen to the man by your side,
Who's had many struggles in his life?
Did you block him out due to troubles of your own?
Did you even ask if he is alone?

Did you notice how broken people seem to be?
Carrying shattered hearts
And grasping onto memories.
Did you even care or is all you do is stare?
Do you help where you can?
Or save yourself from despair?

You can listen, you can help,
You can be someone's light in a world that is broken.
You can be an ear, a heart, a choice.
Britain is broken and it needs a voice.

Your voice, any voice it needs to say,
What's in the hearts of all people today.
Did you hate today? Did you love today?
Did something precious get taken away?

We're you falsely accused, used or abused?
Did you laugh or cry today?
Did a loved one pass away?
Did you notice that child today,

Innocent and full of sun?
Did you just walk by today,
Avoiding everyone?

Were you sacked or made homeless?
Did people bother to say they care?
Did they sit down next to you,
And be present with you there?

Did you get a call today,
Or answer your door?
Or forget about the world outside,
And go back to bed once more?

Did you survive the cold today?
Or have heat from inside?
Did you hear the news you were waiting for?
Did you pray today, thankful you're alive?
I hope you have been blessed today,
And laughed when you could've cried.

Open Your Eyes
by Jules Deason

Take a moment out of your busy day
Just to take in what others say
To look around be more aware
Notice others and show you care.

People rushing with their daily lives
On the other side of the coin
Some people are making the choice to leave or stay
To put money away for a rainy day.

Making decisions to laugh or cry
Is it that hard to open your eyes?
Every heart has a story
Every path leads a different way.

So smile at the stranger
You might just make their day
Take in the beauty around you
When you drown out life's noise.

Open up to a new freedom
Remember to use your voice. Look Up!

The sky is a painting and goes everywhere you go
Feel the depression lifting as you go with the flow.

Hear the music in every day.
When at times life is hopeless
And troubles are in your day
With all the poverty and endless trials
That come your way.

Appreciate the simple things you see
Along your path
So take time for others and offer a friendly heart
As we all need to wake up and this is where it starts.

So run to the sea and along the beach
Count the stars they're not out of reach
Hide in woods go out in the dark
Wait for the lightning with its fiery spark.

Fill all your moments be real and true
And love each other in all you do
Give, share, borrow.
We're not promised tomorrow
Open your eyes beyond reality
Find a new freedom in all you see.

The Sky is a Great Big Green Balloon
by Simon Philbrook

Me and Johnathan
Sat quietly
Looking at the sky
Top of Primrose Hill,
London, all still and whispered
Before us,
Just as I imagined it
From the movies.

Visited his mum
Now eighty
The weight of years
Paint-peeled and dusty
Across her face,
But traces of laughter
Still lingered.

The journey up,
From south of the river
Had been a nightmare,
The tube tugged hard

At his ticks and tricks
Touching any cornered edge
To feel safe.

"They never called it autism
When he was a kid"
His mum had said,
"Just beat him and told me
He was simple".

"He never really talked,
That's how I knew,
At first I thought he caught it
From not knowing his Dad,
Died at Tabruk you know,
I have a medal"

"Later I saw that he was lost
Somewhere in there.
There have been moments…
He'll catch your eye
And say something, and smile.
I know he loves me".

I lie back in the grass
Passing time to let the rush hour go
Before we show our faces to the journey.
Johnathan looks up,
Then half across at me and says
"The sky is a great big green balloon",
I look up
And see it just the same,
"Yes it is" I say.

Yes it is.

Song
by Simon Philbrook

Words without meaning
Are beautifully seductive,
Toys to be played with,
Noises to be sung,
Until the singing
Becomes the song,
And the song
Becomes one
With the raven east wind
And the sunshine sky
So blue it hurts your eyes,
And you finally learn
That poetry is the sound
Of the river trickling in shallows,
And shadows of the moon,
Kiss the ripples
That are all the beauty in the world
Distilled in the sound of their song
And the song is all I need to live,
So I shall live.

Jeff and Sarah
by Craig Neesam

Before I leave this green and blue place
I wanna see and touch your face - Again
That no one round here can replace
But you my friend I saw grace.
Love ya mate.

You were the sun over seaside skies
Held my hand on this road that has no time
And although I cannot see you
I still feel you by my side.
Love ya mate.

So as we sing your sweet name
To the gentleness of the wind
The barrenness of your dying light will never win
For your radiance shines in me, within.
Love ya mate.

And despite death taking your final breath
I hear your warm words
As you said we will always be friends
And with eternity with no end we will meet again.
Love ya mate.

So the seasons may change planets rearrange
But you will stay the same
For your name I will proclaim
No wind nor rain
Could break our galvanised united chain.
Love you mate.

Brighton skies are so blue
And this I know to be true
That you could bounce around any corner
Always new,
But until you do...
I love ya mate.

RIP Jeff Dunning Sarah Lavis.

Memories

by Deirdre Leavy

Memories triggered by something new,
Old pain and hurts come to the forefront
Thinking they were all healed and done with,
That I had seen the last of those old wounds

I realise now they are still there buried,
Still seeping not closed over just
Lying dormant till something stirs them up
Some work I need to do there,
It is time to let them out to heal up fully

I want to be free from the pain,
I am stronger and able to handle them better
Nothing will send me back to a self-destructive path
I have come way too far to let my
Past drag me down the way it used to
Remind yourself of how much
You have grown since then,
How you have changed
Into who you were meant to be

As the triggers come up, now I can look at them,
Deal with them and let them go with love
Each time it gets a little easier and
I am proud of the person I am today

Onwards and upwards
I am free to be the real me

The Way is Lit
by Deirdre Leavy

The way forward is lit,
All those light bulb moments are
Shining lights like beacons for you to follow
Phrases said that make sense now,
Little comments
That flash in your mind opening up new thoughts

You are feeling it deep inside you,
Connecting with your spirit and soul,
It's filling you up with a lightness
That is hard to describe
All the "why didn't I see this sooner"
Fall away as you finally understand
It wasn't meant to be before now

Your journey is yours,
There isn't a time scale for things to happen
When you are ready for it
That is when the time is right
And not a minute sooner

Some need to go slowly taking small steps,
Others take a big leap right off the edge,
There is no right or wrong way,
Only the individual's character
Can determine what is the right way for them

Everyone learns at their own pace,
Everyone feels different fears and worries
Isn't life magical in how it progresses
The beauty of it is that everyone's story
Is just that
Their Story
Their life's journey
Going at exactly the right pace
They are ready for.

Plenty more lightbulb moments will keep coming,
Shining bright, guiding you like little lights
Sparkling, lighting your way

Words are magical all by themselves
With an energy of their own

Once Again Cascade
by Paul Delaware

You are a new spring
Upon a barren mountain.
Soon Cascade you will be
A mighty waterfall.

You bring refreshment
To worldly wanderers,
In their grief
They hear your call.

An inspiration
To those who seek you
And find you, just when
They're about to fall.

That perfect moment of cleansing
Within your meetings
Wherein lies the hope,
To once again stand tall.

Love to Booze to Violence
by Paul Delaware

I look into your eyes and I am lost.
Dreaming romantically in ignorance
Leering perversely with innocence.
Why do your kisses hurt so much?
Why do your punches feel like lust?
Your twisted mind leaves me fumbling all the time,
Babbling out bewildered, broken rhymes.
Is this love or is this crime?
It's impossible to know,
Once you've opened that third bottle of wine.

Sorrow, sorrow now and tomorrow
Why did fate give you such a tragic path to follow.
What happened to your beautiful glowing eyes
That used to lure me in every time?
I guess they were corrupted
By wretched drunken lies.
So now, behind your shallow tears
There's nothing there,
Gaps devoid of any loving care,
All that remains is a withering,
Irked and violent stare.

Extra's

Cross Shadow

Big cross shadow that follows me, above
One arm stretched with a spoon to shove
What is this medicine that burns my mouth?
It sears my throat, want to spit it out

I just want a cuddle to quiet my fear.
A soft word spoken for me to hear.
I'm not alone in this dark room
Stranger's breath will come too soon.

Why are you cross, why do you shout?
I was alone, afraid, I cried out!
Why not stay mam, talk to me
In soothing tones, just you and me.

It no longer burns, my teeth feel strange.
A warming glow from throat to chest
Warm fingers spread from behind my spine.
Soon large hands my body entwined

Lying on Your chest, Your bleeding heart warms.
In Your embrace in heaven swarmed
I sink blissfully into deep deep sleep
This is not real, just the drink!

The effect it has on my small mind
As spoon after spoon you give your child.
You knew no better, I can't blame you.
I'll never know why, it was your tonic too.

Will there be a Song

The flailing dancer within a crippled man.
This solid box, this cage.
Her arms raised, loose headed.
Shouldering this wall then that.
As she shifts, it jolts, the box tilts.
From the waist this naked dancer flops in two,
Arms outstretched
The back of her hands rest on the floor.

Her shoulder meets the wall, her head tilts.
The room lists under her influence.
She is skinny and small.
Her effect affects all.
But the chair-bound man remains
Outwardly unmoved.
Still still he has no choice
The idea of choice has been removed.

He can neither move himself
Nor the dancer within.
But she can move
Buckled knees slide up the incline.

The shadow box moves.
On its axis, now balanced.
She leaps, stamps repeatedly,
Barefooted legs in sync.
Arms like a victorious boxer
She stands.

Getting smaller and smaller.
The box dims.
She is shrouded now
For the grief within.
Behind the veil her light dims.
He can feel the death that beckons
And slowly, quietly she sleeps,
The long sleep.

The crippled man awakes
Feeling anxious and afraid
But not knowing why.
This gaping hole inside,
A yawning chasm nothing can fill it
But her breath.
The smallest lightest of breath.
Her last breath.

For I am the dancer, the box
And the crippled man.
I am the breath that fills
I am the breath that gives
I am the breath that takes
Like gravity, that weak force
That holds planets and stars.
She is the love that affects all.
And I am the Dance.

The dancer is gone
A perceived movement
For a fleeting moment.
But felt so deeply,
At the very core of being.
Now the Dance moves on.
The shadow-box is gone
Now unrestrained
How will you dance.
Will there be another song?

Bass Fishing

Golden sand, beach below
Blues, greens, waves crashing around.
Watching dark depths, currents flow
See the routes, Bass might be found.
Get to the bluff, Stand on the slopes.
On the shore sea breeze blows.
Decided now, pitch our hopes
Looking for where the river flows.

Standing on high, friend beside
In joy shared passion brings.
Fishing now, a sense of pride.
Hoping for Bass and other things

Rod in hand, big long cast.
Arc of line, blue sky, sunshine.
Into the sea with a splash it blasts.
Sinks below tighten in time
In hope now, thumb on line
Feel tension of current and wish.
What might I haul this time.
Big hit, reel in, a specimen fish.

Night descends, tide unwinds.
Moon appears, skimming waves.
Rhythm of sea, wind declines.
Hopes now turning to craves.
Two AM last cast it seems
No weight hitting the sand this time.
Picked on the drop, moon still beams.
I've finally got a Bass this time.

Standing on high, friend beside
In joy shared passion brings.
Fishing now, a sense of pride.
Hoping for Bass and other things.

The Greatest

Bees sting butterflies float.
Who is this black man on which we dote.
Beaming smile a fast chatter.
Big bright eyes the very first rapper.
Full of vim and blessed with vigour.
Another sting as his jab flickers.
Lightning fast with his fists.
Way too pretty for a pugilist.

Mohamed Ali Boom ay yay
Aka Cassius Clay.
Ali boom ay yay,
Aka Cassius Clay.

Don't get involved in a pre-fight bout.
He'll come to your home, scream 'n shout.
He'll mess with your head, mangle your mind.
Only in the prize ring is he unkind.
The rumble in the jungle, Thriller in Manila.
Just no beating this cool clean killer.
Will draw you in Rope a dope
When you're punched out, the butterfly floats.

Mohamed Ali Boom ay yay
Aka Cassius Clay.
Ali boom ay yay,
Aka Cassius Clay.

Was he a chancer, a dancer or a clown?
Doesn't matter he'll mow you down.
Get out of the ring you're in trouble!
His feet in a flurry, the Ali shuffle!
In the segregated states, Ali despairs
Even with the Olympic gold he wears.
Stops in for meal, "We don't serve Negroes here!"
"That's Fine I don't eat 'Em",
But he's shown the door.

Mohamed Ali Boom ay yay
Aka Cassius Clay.
Ali boom ay yay,
Aka Cassius Clay.

He was the greatest and the best
Behind his fists sincere intent
To right the wrongs of slavery.
God hold him close, reward his bravery.

Mohamed Ali Boom ay yay
Aka Cassius Clay.
Ali boom ay yay,
Aka Cassius Clay.

A Word of Thanks

I owe gratitude to:

My beautiful daughters

Nils and all the team at Invisible Voices

Pete Davies and all at Cascade

All at Haga – Haringay action on alcohol, and Kevin
and his team at Shine

Charlotte, for your patience, love and support

Stef O'Driscoll at Nobokov for help and support
writing and with The Story Telling Army project

Roger and all at the Open Mike

Kate McCoy and all at Cascade Drama collective
Washing up project

Elspeth and all at Cascade recovery choir

Molly and all the team at Strummers/New Note

Mike and all at Cascade Wednesday night Writing Group

Janet for editing this manuscript at a moment's notice

David at Haga for the silkscreen portrait.

Simon, what you gave freely, freed me.

And most of all, to my fellow artists some of whom have contributed to this book, and all of whom continue to inspire me on a daily basis.

CASCADE CREATIVE RECOVERY

A community based grassroots charity that helps people who have had a problematic relationship with drugs and/or alcohol to maintain their recovery and discover where they are with their recovery and how they relate to the world.

We run a community coffee shop on Baker Street that provides a safe space. The Coffee Shop is open 6 days a week (closed on Monday) including over holiday periods such as Christmas and Easter. We are peer-led, volunteer run, and use an asset based community development approach.

In addition to the coffee shop we also have popular groups for drama, a choir, walking, craft, and creative writing as tools not only for self-expression but as a way of promoting recovery and making it attractive and exciting.

Along with the Cascade Coffee Shop and our creative activities we also have peer support through Recovery Coaching. A holistic approach to whole person recovery and discovery.

**Cascade Creative Recovery -
Empowering, Informing , Creating.**

INVISIBLE VOICES OF BRIGHTON & HOVE

Invisible Voices of Brighton & Hove was founded in 2016. The aim of this group is to raise awareness regarding local homeless issues, and also to raise funds in support of effective local charities. One way of raising awareness is to give a voice to those who so often remain unheard in our community, by creating an opportunity for vulnerable people to speak out in various ways during the Brighton Fringe Festivals.

For Fringe 2016, we organised a photography exhibition, as well as publishing two books: *Invisible Voices of Brighton & Hove* and *Born and Bred*. The first book being a collection of interviews, journal records, personal stories and poetry, the second poems by street poet extraordinaire Craig Neesam.

For Fringe 2017, we organised another photography exhibition, as well as publishing two further books: *Invisible Voices 2017*, and Craig Neesam's second collection of poems, including contributions by others, called *The Oaks*. We also facilitated a stage show called *Another Brighton*.

For Fringe 2018 there is another photography exhibition, and we have published no less than three books. One is the book you're holding in your hands right now, *The Queen of Brighton*. The second is another book of poetry by the talented young poet Jovannah Bär, entitled *Seasoned Eyes Are Beaming*. The third is called *On Brighton Streets*, which is our first fictional reflection of the local housing crisis. It was written by Cair Going and Nisse Visser, author of the local bestseller *Will's War in Brighton*.

Invisible Voices can be found on Facebook, or our website: www.invisiblevoices.co.uk

www.ingramcontent.com/pod-product-compliance
Lightning Source LLC
Chambersburg PA
CBHW030259130626
46549CB00002B/609